WILD WICKED WONDERFUL

TOP 10:
BITERS

By Virginia Loh-Hagan

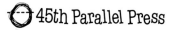

45th Parallel Press

Published in the United States of America by Cherry Lake Publishing
Ann Arbor, Michigan
www.cherrylakepublishing.com

Content Adviser: Stephen Ditchkoff, Professor of Wildlife Ecology and Management, Auburn University, Alabama
Reading Adviser: Marla Conn, ReadAbility, Inc.
Book Designer: Melinda Millward

Photo Credits: ©reptiles4all/ iStockphoto, cover, 1, 10; ©DrC_Photography / iStockphoto, 5; ©devil79sd/Shutterstock Images, 6; ©SW_Stock/Shutterstock Images, 6; ©Shino Iwamura/Shutterstock Images, 6; ©Dori OConnell/ iStockphoto, 7; ©Buffenstein/Barshop Institute/UTHSCSA/http://www.flickr.com/ CC-BY-2.0, 8; ©belizar/Shutterstock Images, 8; © Scott Camazine/Newscom, 9; ©Maria Dryfhout/Shutterstock Images, 10; ©Mark Kostich/ iStockphoto, 10; ©Lakeview Images/Shutterstock Images, 11; ©joloei/ iStockphoto, 12; © Ken Griffiths/NHPA/Photoshot/Newscom, 14; ©James van den Broek/Shutterstock Images, 15; ©worldswildlifewonders/Shutterstock Images, 16; ©Attila JANDI/Shutterstock Images, 17; ©AndreAnita/Shutterstock Images, 18; ©Thomas Quine /http://www.flickr.com/ CC-BY-2.0, 20; ©Michael Lynch/Shutterstock Images, 20; © Dietmar Nill/Nature Picture Library/Corbis, 21; ©photographereddie/ iStockphoto, 22; © 1stGallery/ iStockphoto, 22; ©Victoria Antonova/Shutterstock Images, 22; ©Zuzule/Shutterstock Images, 23; ©sdominick/ iStockphoto, 24; ©dangdumrong/Shutterstock Images, 25; ©G Tipene/Shutterstock Images, 26; ©Richard Susanto/Shutterstock Images, 26; ©Luca Vaime/Shutterstock Images, 26; ©kkaplin/ Shutterstock Images, 27; ©tratong/Shutterstock Images, 28; ©Mogens Trolle/Shutterstock Images, 28; ©EcoPrint/Shutterstock Images, 28; ©GP232/ iStockphoto, 29; ©JSUBiology/http://www.flickr.com/ CC-BY-2.0, 30; © Norbert Wu/Science Faction/Corbis, 30; ©Jerry Kirkhart/http://www.flickr.com/ CC-BY-2.0, 31

Graphic Element Credits: © tukkki/Shutterstock Images, back cover, front cover, multiple interior pages; © paprika/Shutterstock Images, back cover, front cover, multiple interior pages; © Silhouette Lover/Shutterstock Images, multiple interior pages

45th Parallel Press is an imprint of Cherry Lake Publishing.

Library of Congress Cataloging-in-Publication Data

Names: Loh-Hagan, Virginia, author.
   Title: Top 10 : biters / by Virginia Loh-Hagan.
Other titles: Top ten : biters | Biters
Description: Ann Arbor : Cherry Lake Publishing, [2016] | Series: Wild wicked wonderful
Identifiers: LCCN 2015026847| ISBN 9781634705004 (hardcover) | ISBN 9781634706209 (pbk.) |
ISBN 9781634705608 (pdf) | ISBN 9781634706803 (ebook)
Subjects: LCSH: Dangerous animals—Juvenile literature. | Animals—Miscellanea—Juvenile literature.
Classification: LCC QL100 .L646 2016 | DDC 590—dc23
LC record available at http://lccn.loc.gov/2015026847

Printed in the United States of America
Corporate Graphics

About the Author

Dr. Virginia Loh-Hagan is an author, university professor, former classroom teacher, and curriculum designer. She likes biting into cheeseburgers. She lives in San Diego with her very tall husband and very naughty dogs. To learn more about her, visit www.virginialoh.com.

TABLE OF CONTENTS

INTRODUCTION

Animals bite. They bite hard. They use their teeth. They **pierce** another object. Pierce is when a sharp object goes through something.

They bite for different reasons. They bite to protect themselves. They bite to hunt. They bite to hurt. They bite to eat. They bite to play. They bite to warn. They bite to take charge.

Some bites don't break the skin. Some bites cause wounds. **Wounds** are cuts. They bleed. Some bites tear off limbs. Some bites are poisonous. Some bites kill.

Some animals are extreme biters. Their bites are bigger. Their bites are better. They're the most exciting biters in the animal world!

Biting is a natural reaction.

chapter one

MOSQUITOES

Female mosquitoes are insects. They're small. But their bites can be deadly. They want blood. Blood feeds their eggs. Males don't suck blood.

Mosquitoes have special mouthparts. The mouthparts look like tubes. They're like straws. The biting system is special. It's used to suck blood.

They land on skin. They lock in. They dig around. They find blood. They pump out blood. They drink for about four minutes.

Mosquito bites can be itchy!

Their spit sometimes has something in it. It can kill people. It can give people a rash. Mosquito bites can spread sicknesses. Examples are yellow fever and malaria. **Malaria** kills one in 17 people who get it.

Chapter two

NAKED MOLE RATS

Naked mole rats are hairless. They live underground. They live in Africa. They build tunnels. They use their teeth to build. They have strong jaw muscles. They can chew through cement.

They have **buckteeth**. Two front teeth are big. They stick out. They're outside of their lips. This keeps naked mole rats from eating dirt.

Naked mole rats live in a **colony**. This is like a city. One female in the colony is special. She has all the babies. Females fight to be the special one. They bite.

The skin of a naked mole rat doesn't feel pain.

They pierce lungs. They kill. They die.

Naked mole rats protect the colony. Some are soldiers.
They snap. They bite.

chapter three
SNAKES

Most snakes have teeth. They have four rows on the top. They have two rows on the bottom. Snakes don't use teeth to chew food. They use teeth to hunt **prey**. Prey means animals hunted for food.

Some snakes' teeth are like needles. They're called **fangs**. Fangs are long, sharp teeth. They make holes in skin. They dig deep. They inject poison.

Snakes don't always have their fangs out. They fold their fangs against the roof of their mouths. This is so they don't bite themselves. They strike. Then their fangs come out.

The worst snake biters live in Australia.

Snakes' teeth break. They wear out. Snakes grow new teeth. They're always ready to attack.

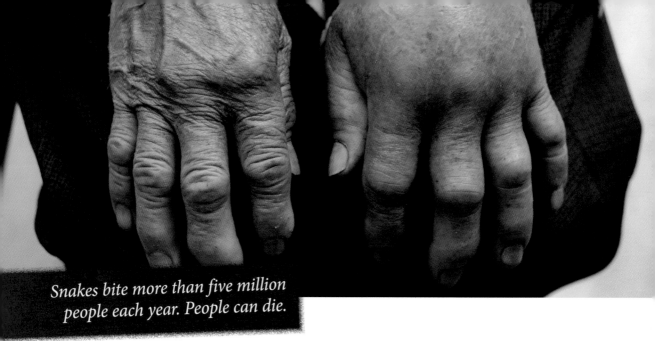

Snakes bite more than five million people each year. People can die.

Snake teeth can be found in their poop. The teeth get stuck in prey. Snakes eat the prey. The teeth pass through their bodies.

Snakes bite to defend themselves. They have pits on the sides of their faces. These pits feel heat. They feel living things. Snakes bite things that get too close.

Snakes still bite after they die. Even if snakes get chopped in half. Snake heads will keep biting. Their nerves still work.

Snakes have a strong bite **reflex**. It's an instant movement. They just bite once. They bite quickly. Then they move away. Their bites take less than a second.

DID YOU KNOW...?

- Some people milk killer spiders. They're developing an antidote. An antidote is medicine for poison.

- Crocodiles fought in World War II. The British surrounded the Japanese army on an island. One thousand men tried to escape. They swam through swamps. Crocodiles were in the swamps. They attacked. They killed many men.

- Hippopotamus teeth are made of ivory. They're similar to elephant tusks. Hippo ivory does not turn yellow. It was used to make George Washington's fake teeth.

- Cookiecutter sharks attacked a submarine. A submarine is an underwater boat. The sharks bit into pieces of rubber on the submarine. They damaged the submarine. It had to go back to base for repairs.

- Hagfish look like eels. They have tentacles around their mouths. Tentacles are like flexible arms. Hagfish eat dead animals. They have two rows of teeth. They bury their faces in the dead animals. They bite off meat chunks.

Chapter four
FUNNEL WEB SPIDERS

Funnel web spiders live in Australia. They strike super quickly. They have big fangs. Their fangs point straight down. They're strong. They bite through a lizard's skull. They bite through human fingernails. They bite through shoes.

These spiders don't have jaws. Their fangs are connected to their mouths. The fangs aren't used for chewing. They're used for killing prey. They throw up special spit. This turns their prey into soup. Then they suck it up.

Funnel web spiders are one of the world's most dangerous spiders.

The spiders' bites are really poisonous to humans. People have died. Spiders inject poison. Their prey can't move.

chapter five

CROCODiLES

Crocodiles have powerful jaws. Their jaws have many muscles. They slam shut. Their bite is strong. It's 10 times stronger than a human's bite.

Crocodiles have 60 to 80 teeth. They replace their teeth. They do it about 50 times before they die. Their teeth are shaped like cones. They're sharp. They pierce skin. But they can't tear flesh. They grab their prey. They hold the prey. They drive their teeth into them. Prey can't escape.

Most of a crocodile's jaw muscles are for clamping down.

Crocodiles wait for prey to get close to the water's edge.

Crocodiles can hold their breath. They can do this for about an hour. They attack without warning. They eat anything that floats into their mouths. They kill about 2,000 humans a year.

Humans Do What?!?

Luis Suárez is a soccer player. He bit his opponent's arm. In another game, he bit an opponent's shoulder. He's not the only biting athlete. Jermain Defoe is a soccer player. He bit his opponent's arm. Johan le Roux is a rugby player. He bit his opponent's ear. The most famous biting athlete is Mike Tyson. He's a boxer. He bit off a chunk of Evander Holyfield's left ear. He tried to bite his other ear. The boxing match was stopped. They were competing for the world heavyweight title. Tyson was disqualified. He was not allowed to box. He had to pay $3 million. Their boxing match is called the "Bite Fight." Biting can happen in contact sports. Human bites can be more dangerous than most animal bites. There are germs in human mouths. They sometimes cause infections that are hard to treat.

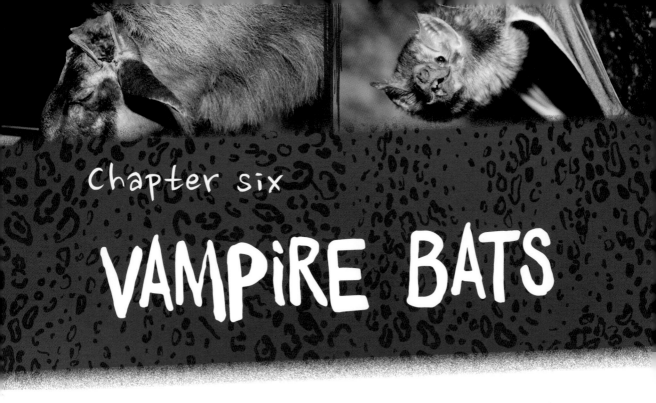

Chapter Six

VAMPIRE BATS

Vampire bats live in Central and South America. They hunt at night. They find sleeping victims. They find a warm spot on the skin. They use their teeth. They shave away hairs or fur. They make a small cut. They suck at the wound. They drink blood. They do it without waking their prey.

Their spit is special. It makes their victims bleed. It makes their prey **numb**. Numb means being unable to feel anything.

Their front teeth are for cutting. They're really sharp. Their back teeth are smaller than other bats. They also have fewer

A part of a vampire bat's brain detects sleeping victims.

teeth. They don't use their teeth to chew food. Their tongue has a groove. It laps up their bloody meal.

chapter seven

DOGS

There are more than 50 million dogs in the United States. They live happily with humans. But some can be dangerous. There's a one in 50 chance of being bitten each year. Dogs bite over 4.7 million Americans each year.

Dog bites draw blood. Dogs are most dangerous to children. Children are at their same height.

Dog bites can be deadly. Dog bites are more dangerous than bites from bears, alligators, and spiders combined! Dog spit has germs. Some dog bites cause **rabies**. Rabies

Dogs are our pets. But they're also animals.

is a bad sickness. It kills more than 55,000 people a year around the world. Dog bites are mostly to blame.

Even little dogs and puppies can bite hard enough to kill babies and small children.

Biting dogs have a lot of speed. They have good aim. They have strong jaws. They have sharp teeth. They don't let go. They can tear muscles and skin. They can bite through chests. They can damage organs.

There are different levels of dog bites. Level 1 is when dogs snap. Or they bite air. They do not touch humans. This is how they warn. Level 2 is when a dog's teeth make contact with skin. But there's no wound. Level 3 is when dogs bite more than once. There are wounds. But the wounds aren't deep. Level 4 means the wounds are deep. When they bite, dogs shake their heads. This is a serious bite. Level 5 is when dogs bite several times. The wounds are deep. Level 6 is when dogs kill someone. Or they've eaten flesh.

WHEN ANIMALS ATTACK!

A Washington State woman sent her dog out to use the bathroom. The dog was in a fenced yard. It barked in pain. A large raccoon was on top of it. The dog had back and leg wounds. A week later, six raccoons attacked a neighbor's cat. Raccoons in the wild are not dangerous. They leave humans and animals alone. But more raccoons are living in cities. They are not hunted. They eat humans' trash. Raccoons have hurt humans, too. An 88-year-old woman in Connecticut let her cat in. A raccoon followed the cat. The woman petted it by mistake. The raccoon had rabies. It bit her elbow, hand, arm, lip, and chin. She called the police. The raccoon attacked two policemen. A baby in Michigan was attacked by a raccoon. It took off her nose and ear. Humans need to keep raccoons away. One way is to spray coyote urine, lemon juice, or vinegar.

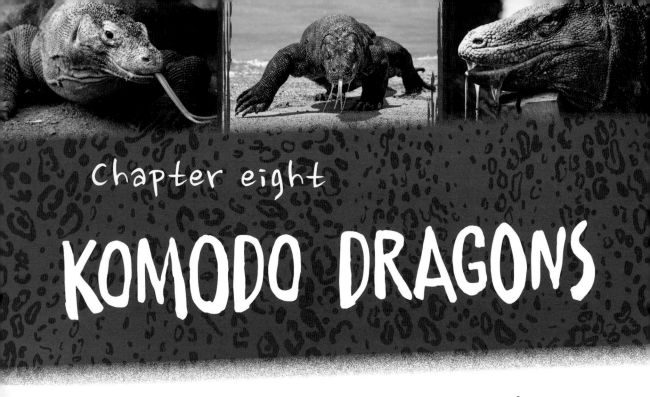

chapter eight

KOMODO DRAGONS

Komodo dragons live in Indonesia. They're like giant lizards. They can bring down big animals. They can do it in one bite. They have very bad breath. Meat gets trapped in their mouths. Their spit has many germs. One bite poisons the blood.

Komodo dragons have more than 60 teeth. Their teeth are sharp. They're **serrated**. They have jagged edges. They look like saws. They're deadly.

Komodo dragons will eat almost anything. They'll eat humans. They wait for their prey. They attack the throat.

Komodo dragons eat a lot in one feeding. They can skip many meals.

They wait for the poison to kill the prey. They tear large chunks of flesh. They swallow whole. They throw up horns, hair, and teeth.

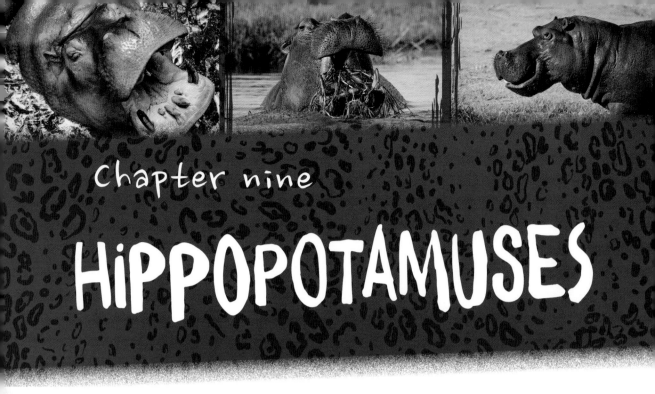

Chapter nine

HiPPOPOTAMUSES

Hippos live in Africa. They kill more people in the wild than other animals. They don't eat people. They chew them up. They attack boats. They fight other hippos. They kill. They do it in one bite.

Hippos are very **territorial**. They guard their space. They protect their babies. But sometimes, they attack for no reason.

They open their jaws wide. Their jaws open more than 4 feet (122 centimeters). Males have sharp teeth. Their teeth can grow up to 28 inches (71 cm) long. They use their front

Hippos eat plants. But some hippos kill other hippos.

teeth. They block attacks. They use their teeth to attack.
Hippos have more bite force than a shark.

chapter ten
COOKIECUTTER SHARKS

Cookiecutter sharks are also called cigar sharks. They're small. They're about 22 inches (56 cm) long.

Compared to their size, they have the largest teeth of any shark. They have about 30 bottom teeth. Their bottom teeth are large. They're shaped like triangles. They have about 40 upper teeth. Their upper teeth are smaller. They're straight. All their teeth have straight edges.

They lose their teeth in whole rows. They replace the teeth all at once. They eat them.

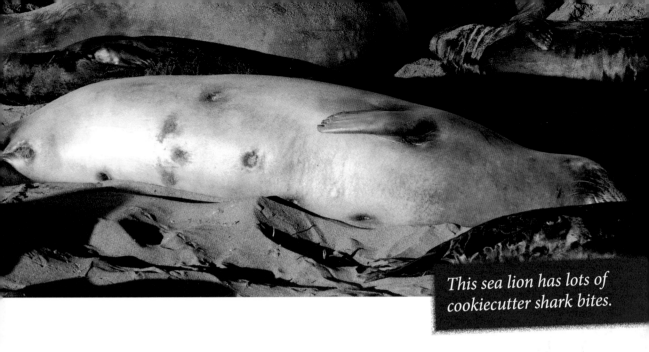

This sea lion has lots of cookiecutter shark bites.

They're always looking for prey. They hunt bigger animals. They hunt whales, seals, and other sharks.

Cookiecutter sharks use their tongues. They use their lips. They suck into the prey. They sink in their upper teeth. This holds them to the prey. They use their lower teeth to saw. They slice into the prey. They twist. They spin their bodies. They make a circle. Their jaws go back and forth. They scoop out a chunk of flesh.

They eat and run. They swim off. They leave behind wounds. The wounds are about 2 inches (5 cm) wide. They're about 3 inches (7.6 cm) deep. They're shaped like cones. They look like cookies. It's like the shark used a cookie cutter.

CONSIDER THIS!

TAKE A POSITION! Should animals that attack humans be put to death? Argue your point with reasons and evidence.

SAY WHAT? In chapter seven, you learned about different levels of dog bites. There are also different types of spider bites. Learn about them. Explain the different spider bites.

THINK ABOUT IT! Biting is a natural reaction. Young children bite. Why do they bite?

LEARN MORE!

- Stout, Frankie. *Nature's Nastiest Biters*. New York: PowerKids Press, 2008.
- Winters, Kari-Lynn, and Ishta Mercurio. *Bite into Bloodsuckers*. Markham, ON: Fitzhenry and Whiteside, 2015.

GLOSSARY

buckteeth (buhk-TEETH) big front teeth that stick out

colony (KAH-luh-nee) an organization like a city with leaders and workers

fangs (FANGZ) long, sharp teeth at the sides of the mouth

malaria (muh-LAIR-ee-uh) a disease spread by mosquitoes

numb (NUHM) unable to feel anything

pierce (PEERS) when a sharp object goes through something

prey (PRAY) animals that are hunted for food

rabies (RAY-beez) a disease spread by animals

reflex (REE-fleks) instant movement, reaction

serrated (SER-ay-tid) jagged

territorial (ter-i-TOR-ee-uhl) protective

wounds (WOONDZ) open cuts

INDEX